Women Too!

All I Want Is a Baby   3
The Greatest   9
The Women's Story   15
Keep Your Wig On, Judge!   21
'Sunday Trading'   28

Bible stories retold by
Michael Forster

First published in 1997 by
KEVIN MAYHEW LTD
Rattlesden
Bury St Edmunds
Suffolk IP30 0SZ

© 1997 Michael Forster

The right of Michael Forster to be identified as the author of this work has been asserted by him in accordance with the Copyright, Designs and Patents Act 1988.

All rights reserved. No part of this publication may be reproduced, stored in a retrieval system, or transmitted, in any form or by any means, electronic, mechanical, photocopying, recording or otherwise, without the prior written permission of the publisher.

The stories in this book are extracted from *A story, a hug and a prayer* (© 1994 Kevin Mayhew Ltd), *Good night, God bless* (© 1995 Kevin Mayhew Ltd) and *God bless, sleepy head* (© 1997 Kevin Mayhew Ltd).

0 1 2 3 4 5 6 7 8 9

ISBN 1 84003 024 0
Catalogue No 1500128

Cover by Eddy Mooney
Typesetting by Louise Hill
Printed and bound in Great Britain

All I Want Is a Baby

Once there lived a man called Elkanah, who had two wives. Men were allowed to do that in those days, but no one had heard of women's liberation, so women could only have one husband – and often they had to share him.

One of Elkanah's wives was called Hannah and the other was called Pennina, which is a very nice name for someone who wasn't a very nice person. She'd had lots of children, and in those days people thought that that made you very special. Hannah had no children, which meant that everyone looked down on her. Hannah was very unhappy, because she longed for a child of her own.

What made things worse was that Pennina kept on sneering at Hannah. 'You've got no children,' she would say. 'You're useless – can't even do a simple thing like that.'

Elkanah didn't help, either. Whenever the big festivals came round, he always gave lots more presents to Pennina than to Hannah. Of course, he would never admit that he loved Pennina more. He would try to explain by saying, 'She needs more than you do, with all those children of hers.' And that just made Hannah feel even worse! What a silly thing to say!

One day, when Hannah was really upset and was crying, Elkanah tried to comfort her; but he wasn't very good at that kind of thing and whenever he opened his mouth he put his foot in it.

'Why are you crying?' he said. 'I know you've got no children, but that doesn't matter. After all, who needs children, when you've got me!'

That hadn't come out quite the way Elkanah meant it to, but Hannah didn't seem to notice; she was just angry. She got up and ran out of the house. Elkanah started to run after her, but he was a bit out of condition and soon gave up.

Hannah ran to the place of worship. She was really upset and needed somewhere quiet to think. After she had been there a little while, she started praying. She didn't pray out loud, but just whispered the words so that no one else could hear. 'God,' she said, 'I really want to have a baby – I've always wanted one. If you let me have a child, I promise I'll nurse him well, and then as soon as he can eat ordinary food I'll give him to you. I won't mind – honestly – I'll be happy knowing I've got a child, even if I can't see him and play with him. I just want to be a mother.'

You may wonder why she assumed that the baby would be a boy. Well, that's just the way people thought and spoke in those days. It was a man's world even before he'd been born! Come to that, a lot of people still think that kind of way now!

Anyway, back to Hannah. What she didn't know was that there was an old priest called Eli standing watching her. He could see her lips moving, but no words were coming out.

'Oh dear!' he thought. 'Another drunk. They think they can come in here to shelter from the rain, and they always end up embarrassing me.' So he went over to Hannah. 'I think you'd better leave,' he said. Hannah didn't know he was talking to her, and just kept on praying. So Eli tried again.

'Did you hear what I said? Out!'

Hannah still carried on praying, until she felt her shoulder being shaken. 'Come on,' said the priest. 'I said out! It really is too much. You people come in here, getting in the way, annoying the paying – I mean praying public.'

'Oh no, sir,' said Hannah. 'I'm not drunk, just terribly unhappy.' And with that, she burst into tears.

Underneath all his priestly dignity, Eli actually had a very gentle heart. He put his arm around Hannah and tried to comfort her. 'I'm sorry,' he said, 'but we have to be careful here, you know. Do you want to talk about it?'

Hannah told him the whole story. Eli was very angry and began to raise his voice. 'Someone ought to give that Pennina woman a good talking to!' he bellowed. 'And where's your husband? I'll give him a lesson in sensitivity!'

'Oh, no, please don't do that,' said Hannah. 'They're not bad people, really – and I do have

All I Want Is a Baby 7

to live with them afterwards, you know. Don't worry – I've said my prayer, and now I'll have to leave it to God.'

Eli smiled. 'Well, you may be right,' he said. 'Off you go home, and try not to worry. I've been working for God for quite a long time, and he hasn't let me down yet.'

After that, Hannah seemed happier. Pennina couldn't annoy her with her snide remarks about children any more, so she changed her tactics.

'You're putting on weight,' she said one day. 'Elkanah won't like that. And it's not as if you've got any excuse, is it? I mean, I've still got my figure even after having *all those children*.'

Hannah just smiled mysteriously. She had a pretty good idea why she was putting on weight, and she was very happy about it.

Sure enough, a few months later Hannah had her baby. It was a beautiful little boy, and she called him Samuel. Elkanah was over the moon. He was so proud of Hannah he could hardly stand still. 'My son,' he said. 'He's going to be a really great man – perhaps a farmer, or a camel driver.'

'No, he's not,' said Hannah. 'I promised him to God. And just as soon as he can feed for himself, I'm going to take him to the priest.'

Based on 1 Samuel 1:1-20

THE GREATEST

Susie's mum and dad were talking about Important Matters. And that meant Susie wasn't included in the conversation, but she was used to that. Whenever there was anything interesting happening, she got left out. Her parents were always very kind about it.

'One day, you'll be a woman,' her father explained. 'Then you'll understand and be able to join in.'

'But how will I understand when I'm grown up if I don't get a chance to learn?' she asked.

Dad smiled in that annoying way parents have when they don't want children to know they're stuck for an answer. 'You'll understand when you're older,' he asserted, and went back to his Serious Conversation with Mum.

'I still think we should book Tuney Tim,' said Mum. 'Sally and James said he was wonderful at little Tom's party; he sang some lovely songs.'

'Maybe,' replied Dad, 'but I've heard Mystery Mick the conjuror is really great. They had him next door for Rachel's tenth birthday. I think he'd be just right for Susie.'

'Well, I think . . .' Susie started to say.

'Not now, Susie, dear,' said Mum in her special patronising voice. 'Daddy and Mummy are very busy planning your lovely party, so why not just play with your nice little toys and let us get on with it.'

Susie cringed. When were they going to stop treating her like a baby? And whose party was it anyway?

Dad gave her another of those smiles and said, 'Mummy and Daddy know what's best.'

That, Susie told herself, was what *they* thought. She knew all about Tuney Tim. Most of her friends had had him for their party recently, because all the mums and dads loved him. Well, of course they would, wouldn't they? He was the same age as them, and he sang all the silly nursery rhymes they remembered. And as for that conjuror! Everyone knew how all those old tricks were done, but the parents thought the children were being fooled by it! Susie and her friends knew exactly what was going on, of course: their parties were being hijacked so that parents who were sorry they'd ever grown up could pretend to be children again – and it wasn't fair!

Just as Susie was wondering what to do, the mum from next door came bursting in, all excited. 'Guess what!' she said. 'Jesus is here. He's holding a meeting just up the hill.'

Mum and Dad jumped up as though they'd been stung. 'Jesus?' echoed Dad. 'We've got to go and hear him. Susie: shoes!'

'Oh, great!' thought Susie, grimly. 'What's he, a juggler or something?' But she knew it was no good arguing with her parents because they'd only say that They Knew Best. So she put her shoes on and went out with them.

When they got to the place, she saw a man standing apart from the rest and talking to the crowd that was gathering. It was worse than a juggler: it was a preacher! This was one time Susie didn't mind when her parents told her to stay at the edge of the crowd. 'You can play with all your nice little friends,' Mum cooed. 'Won't that be lovely!' And Susie was put in a group of children being cared for by a fifty-five-year-old child with a bad memory.

Susie was just thinking how boring this was when she heard voices being raised. People were getting cross with each other, and that usually meant something interesting was going to happen. So Susie pricked up her ears. She recognised her dad's voice.

'All this is all very well, Jesus, but the point is who're the *really important* people going to be, when you're in power?'

Trust Dad. Always on about importance and power! Susie was about to look away again when she heard Jesus say, 'Bring me one of those children.'

'Oh dear,' thought Susie, 'another entertainer. What's it going to be: "Pick a card" or "What's that in your ear"?' Susie had had so many strange objects fished out of her ear by magicians it was getting seriously boring, and she knew they really had them in their hands the whole time.

The Greatest 13

The trick was always to watch the hand they were trying to distract you from. To her horror, Susie found herself being grasped by the arm and dragged out to the front. 'Mustn't keep Jesus waiting!' muttered Dad. 'He's an Important Person.' And suddenly, Susie was standing in the middle of the crowd.

'Here's one of the most important people in God's world,' said Jesus. Susie looked around to see who Jesus meant, but everyone else was looking back at her! Jesus continued, 'God's not interested in cleverness, but in faith and humility. This is what you've all got to be like if you want to be Really Important. Now, why are all those children being kept out? Get them into the middle!'

Suddenly, Jesus was surrounded by children, of all ages, and Susie found herself being talked to like a ten-year-old instead of a baby! Jesus seemed able to find just the right way to talk to all the children, but more importantly than that, he *listened* to them just as carefully. He really seemed to be interested in what each child thought. And he never said, 'You're Too Young To Understand,' once!

All too soon, it was time to go, but Susie had an idea. 'Please Jesus,' she said, 'will you come to my birthday party?'

'Of course, I will!' replied Jesus. 'It's an honour to be invited.' He turned to Susie's parents. 'Will that be alright?'

Dad smiled. 'I wouldn't dare say no!' he answered. Then he turned to Susie. 'You'd better come home, now,' he said, 'because we're going to need your help to choose the best kind of food.'

Based on Matthew 18:1-7

THE WOMEN'S STORY

This is the story of Mary. She lived a very long time ago in a town called Nazareth. Yes, that's right – *that* Mary. She wasn't very old – perhaps sixteen or thereabouts – but in those days girls got married very young, and people were beginning to talk. 'What about Mary?' they used to say. 'She's on the shelf you know – should be married and have a family by now.'

Sometimes, people used to say even nastier things like, 'After all, having babies is what women are for, isn't it? And if she can't get a husband there's no way she can do that.' The trouble was that even people who didn't say that kind of thing sometimes still thought it, deep down. Where Mary came from, women weren't thought to be very important – and if they hadn't got a husband then they weren't important at all. But God was about to change all of that, as we shall see later.

Mary used to get upset, sometimes, about the cruel things people said about her, but the person she was really sorry for was her cousin Elizabeth. Elizabeth was much older than Mary, and married, and yet she didn't have any children. If Mary ever asked about that, Elizabeth just used to say, 'If I were going to have any children, it would have happened by now. No, I expect you'll be a mother before I am, at this rate.'

So of course, when people weren't gossiping about Mary they were being unkind to Elizabeth. 'Not much of a wife, is she?' they used to say. 'Can't even give her husband a baby.'

Mary was very sad about that, and every time she prayed she asked God to help her cousin Elizabeth to have a baby.

One day, Mary was doing some work around the house. There was a broken chair and she knew that if she waited for her father to mend it then it would never be done, so she went and found some tools and some glue and settled down to work. Just as she got to a very tricky part of the job, she heard a voice say, 'Hello, Mary.'

'That's strange,' thought Mary. 'I'm not expecting any visitors.' She didn't want to look up in case she let her hand slip and ruined her work, so she just kept her head down and carried on. 'It must have been the wind,' she thought to herself.

Then the voice came again: 'Mary.'

This time Mary knew it must be real, but she didn't want to lose track of her work. So she kept her head down and her eye on what she was doing, and said, 'Hello. Who's that?'

'I'm the Archangel Gabriel,' said the voice.

Mary was just about to say, 'Yes, and I'm the queen of Sheba,' when something made her look up – and there he was! Mary was speechless at first. I mean, what do you say to an angel? Normally, she would have offered any visitor a seat and some food and drink, but she didn't know whether angels needed those things or not. Anyway, she hadn't finished mending the chair, yet.

When Mary eventually found her voice, all the words just fell over one another.

'Very pleased to meet you, I'm sure,' she said. 'I'm sorry that I ignored you just now, but I've just got to the tricky bit. If you want my parents, I'm afraid they're both out but if you come back about six you can see them, or of course you can talk to me but I'm sure you want someone more important. The Rabbi lives just down the road, and . . .'

'Mary! Mary!' said Gabriel. 'Let me get a word in edgeways. It's *you* I've come to see. I've been sent to tell you that God's very pleased with you. He thinks you're a very special person.'

'Oh, it's nothing really,' said Mary. 'Anyone can mend a chair if they really want to.'

'Not that,' said Gabriel. 'You're going to have a baby. He's going to be a great ruler and save the world. He'll be known as the Son of God, and he'll rule for ever.'

Now if Mary hadn't known he was an angel she'd have laughed, but instead she just said, 'Me? Have a baby? That's a bit difficult for a single girl, isn't it?'

'Not for God,' said Gabriel. 'If God's decided to use you in a special way, why should he need a man to help him?'

'Well, it's usual' said Mary. 'At least where having babies is concerned.'

'Nothing's impossible for God,' said Gabriel. 'You know your cousin Elizabeth, who's never been able to have a baby?'

'Yes,' said Mary. 'Everyone thinks she's no good because of that.'

'It's certainly a very unfair world, isn't it?' said Gabriel. 'Women seem to get the blame for everything. Anyway, she's going to have a baby as well – she's six months pregnant. So don't you go saying that anything's impossible where God's concerned.'

Mary was a bit lost for words. Obviously something absolutely stunning was happening, and all she could think of to say was, 'Well, God's the boss – whatever he wants is OK by me.'

'Good,' said Gabriel. 'That's what he hoped you'd say.'

As soon as Gabriel had gone, Mary threw away the chair she was mending and all the bits fell apart again, but she was too excited to bother with mending a silly old chair! After all, any man can do that, but they can't have babies, can they! Mary went to get her coat and scarf, and then she ran out of the house and all the way to her cousin Elizabeth's place. They were so happy – they hugged one another, and they danced and sang, and were completely

overjoyed. God had chosen both women for a special purpose, and no one could ever look down on either of them any more. It had always been a silly thing to do, anyway – hadn't it!

Based on Luke 1:26-40

Keep Your Wig On, Judge!

Gabriella's husband had died and she was left alone with her daughter, Becky. In those days women's jobs were not very well paid at all, and even if she could get a good job Gabriella couldn't leave Becky on her own while she went to work. So how were they going to pay the rent?

Sam, the landlord, had always seemed a nice man. That was when Gabriella's husband was alive, though – when the rent was being paid each week. Sam was one of those people who was always very nice to anyone who had money to spend, but changed completely if they fell on hard times. So when Gabriella went to see him he was not very helpful.

'It's not my fault your husband's dead, is it?' he said, nastily. 'I've still got to live you know. I've got to pay my butler, and the man who prunes my roses, and of course I only drink the very best wine. So I can't go reducing people's rent or I might end up poor and pathetic like you.'

Gabriella was really upset. 'I thought you were a friend,' she cried.

'Look, sister,' sneered Sam, 'there are no friends in business. And this is business. You find the money, or I'll find another tenant – one who won't whinge all the time.'

Gabriella didn't know what to do. She was really angry with Sam, but she knew that if she didn't find the money then she and Becky would have nowhere to live. So she tried to earn the money. For a time she got a job fruit picking, but she knew that once the season was over that would come to an end. Then she heard about a job as a cleaner at the local tailor's. The work was quite hard – Gabriella was always getting hurt by needles and scissors that were left lying around – and it was very badly paid. Also, she had to take Becky along with her, and she didn't think that was either safe or fair.

One day Becky said to her mother, 'If you didn't have to pay so much rent, you wouldn't need to earn so much money.'

Gabriella smiled. How wonderful it must be

to be a child, and to see everything in such simple ways, she thought. If only Becky knew what a complicated world it really was! 'The trouble is,' she explained, 'that Sam owns most of the houses in the town and so he can charge what he likes.'

That afternoon, when they were out for a walk, they saw a man who was wearing really funny clothes. Becky thought he looked silly – especially since he was wearing a wig. 'Hasn't he got any hair of his own?' she asked.

'Yes,' laughed Gabriella, 'but he's a very important person. He's a judge.'

'Oh,' said Becky. 'Does that mean that the more important people are, the more silly they have to look?'

Gabriella thought that Becky might have a point, but she was teaching her daughter to be polite, so she said, 'You mustn't talk like that about people. He probably thinks that your clothes are silly, but he hasn't said so.'

'What does a judge do, then?' asked Becky.

'Oh,' said her mother, 'he settles arguments

between people. If someone's being unfair to someone else then he can tell them to stop.'

Before Gabriella could stop her, Becky was running over to the judge.

'Hey, mister Judgy person,' she called out. 'Can you help my mum, please, and stop Sam charging her so much rent – and I promise I won't say your wig looks silly ever again.'

The judge, who knew just how important he was and wanted everyone else to know it as well, stopped and looked first at Becky and then at Gabriella. 'Is this abominable child your responsibility?' he shouted. 'Take her home and punish her – and teach her to be polite to important people, you disgusting, scruffy woman.'

'She's not abominable,' said Gabriella, 'and if I'm scruffy it's because I do an honest job. Anyway, I'd rather be scruffy than rude and arrogant. Come on, Becky.'

Gabriella was surprised at herself. Who would ever have thought that she would speak to a judge like that? 'I shouldn't have done that,' she said to Becky. 'We must always be polite.

Just because someone's rude to you doesn't mean you can be rude back.'

'You weren't rude,' said Becky. 'You were just standing up for yourself. Anyway, I think he should help you.'

Gabriella started thinking about what Becky had said. Perhaps she should go and see the judge.

'Why should I help you?' the judge said. 'You're the rude woman with the horrible child, aren't you?'

'I'm sorry if you think I was rude,' said Becky, 'but you weren't very polite, either. Anyway what you think of me doesn't alter the case. I'm being charged too much rent.'

'Go away,' said the Judge. 'Sam is a good respectable citizen. And he's very rich. We need rich people in this town a lot more than we need characters like you.'

That did it. Gabriella decided the judge was going to do the right thing, if it took her the rest of her life to make him do it. Every day, she went to his house and knocked on his door, but he wouldn't see her. Then she made a big poster saying, 'Sack the unjust judge' and went and stood outside his courtroom with it. Soon she was joined by other women, and every time the judge went past they started chanting, 'Fair rents for all'.

Eventually, it all got too much for the judge, and he called Sam to see him at his courtroom. 'You'll have to lower your rents,' he said.

'Not me,' said Sam. 'Anyway, if I do that, I'll have less to pay you.'

'Shut up!' hissed the judge. 'Do you want the whole town to hear? Look, I've had enough of being pestered by these women. Either you reduce your rents or we'll get the inspectors in to check your houses over.'

'Oh, don't do that!' said Sam, hastily. 'I'll cut the rents.'

The judge went and told the women. 'Now will you leave me alone?' he asked.

'Well,' said Gabriella, 'we're very pleased about the rents, but we think we ought to talk to you about fair wages for cleaners.'

Based on Luke 18:2-5

'Sunday Trading'

Rachel was not at all happy. She had been ill for eighteen years! It was a strange illness that made it impossible for her to stand up. She had been to lots of doctors, but none of them could help. They'd tried all kinds of things, but nothing worked. Now, she had almost no money left and it looked as though she was going to be bent double for the rest of her life. It was a great shame, because she used to be very fit at one time, going for long walks, swimming in the rivers and lakes and even taking part in the town's annual 'Donkey Derby'! Now, she had had to stop doing all those things and rely on other people to help her. Even simple things like hanging out the washing were impossible, because she couldn't reach the line. The worst thing was that she wasn't particularly old, but life seemed to have lost all its meaning for her. She longed to be able to walk upright like other people and perhaps play some games with the children. She couldn't even look up and see the sky without a great effort.

One Saturday, she was in the synagogue at worship. In those days, Saturday was rather like our Sunday. It was called the 'Sabbath', which means it was set aside for people to rest. People went to the synagogue to worship God and no-one was allowed to do any work which was not really necessary. They were very strict about that – some people thought a little too strict. It was good to have a day of rest, of course, and it was good for almost everyone to rest on the same day, because it meant that life was quieter. So everybody was happy with that. The trouble was that the people who made the laws had made it so strict that it sometimes got silly. You couldn't even go and see your friends, if they lived any distance away, because walking counted as work, unless it was to the synagogue of course! This particular day, Jesus was teaching in the synagogue, and he saw Rachel come in, all bent double, and obviously in pain. So he went over to her, to see whether he could help.

'What's the matter?' Jesus asked, 'Can't you stand up straight?' 'I haven't stood up straight for eighteen years!' replied Rachel, and then added, 'And even if I could I'd keep my head down in this place.' 'Why's that?' asked Jesus. 'Well,' said Rachel, 'we women don't have much of a place in the synagogues do we? Even if I could stand up straight, I'd probably be frightened to, in case someone noticed me!' 'That's silly,' said Jesus, 'everyone should be able to hold their head up proudly in God's house.' And as he said it, he took her by the hand and lifted her up. And do you know what happened? Her back straightened, her head came up, and she looked right into Jesus' eyes! Everyone was amazed and a lot of them were very pleased. But there was at least one person who wasn't. Jerry, the leader of the synagogue was angry. He *said* he was cross with Jesus for 'working' on the Sabbath day, but some people thought it was other things he was really worried about. Some people, like him, just didn't like Jesus very much and were always trying to catch him out. 'You've broken the law,' he said to Jesus, 'you've worked on the day of rest.' 'You can't

'Sunday Trading' 31

call that work,' said Jesus, 'all I did was take her hand and help her to stand up straight. Don't you want her to be able to stand up straight in God's house?' 'That's not the point,' said Jerry, 'we all know you're a healer – so healing is work and you shouldn't do it on a rest day. You've got the other six days for doing that.' Jesus thought this was really very silly indeed, and very cruel. 'What if she was a farm animal who had fallen into a well?' he asked, 'Would it be alright for me to go and pull her out?' 'That's different,' shouted Jerry, getting very angry. 'The law says you can do that, because it's an emergency.' 'So,' said Jesus, 'the law thinks that a farm animal is more important than a woman!' Everyone laughed at that – except for Jerry, who just got more and more angry, because people like that don't like being laughed at, at all!

Jesus went on, and said, 'You can rescue animals on the rest day, and you can feed them, so of course, a woman who's had to put up with illness for eighteen years should be freed from it on the same day! She's just as important as you or anyone else, and don't you ever forget it.' Jerry could not find any answer to that and he was very embarrassed. The rest of the people were really overjoyed. 'That was the best service we've been to for a long time,' many of them said – and that just made Jerry jump up and down all the more!

As for Rachel, she went home, singing and dancing as she went, looking up at the beautiful blue sky and stopping to play with every child she met on the way. From now on, life was going to be very different indeed!

Based on Luke 13:10-17